My First Science Book

by Jacqueline McCann

ARCTURUS

ARCTURUS

This edition published in 2019 by Arcturus Publishing Limited
26/27 Bickels Yard, 151–153 Bermondsey Street,
London SE1 3HA

Author: Jacqueline McCann
Consultant: Helen Lewis
Illustrator: Samantha Meredith
Designer: Ms Mousepenny
Editor: Sebastian Rydberg

ISBN: 978-1-78888-506-5
CH006570US
Supplier 29, Date 0519, Print run 7889

Printed in China

What is STEM?

STEM is a world-wide initiative
that aims to cultivate an
interest in Science, Technology,
Engineering, and Mathematics,
in an effort to promote these
disciplines to as wide a variety of
students as possible.

Contents

Welcome to My First Science Book

Hello,

Are you curious and interested in the world around you? Do you like to explore living things? Then you are a young scientist!

This book is divided into four different sections that show you science is all around you.

There are fun activities and puzzles on every other page. When you've finished them, check the answers at the back of the book to see how you did.

Have fun!

Amazing Plants

You'll discover how many kinds of plants there are in the world and where they grow. You'll find out what the different parts of a plant are called and how they fit together. How do plants make new plants? Turn to this section to find out.

Awesome Animals

Some animals fly in the sky, live on the earth, or crawl underground. Others swim in the sea or move between water and land. You're an animal too—where do you like to be? Learn about the different parts of your body and how to keep it in good working order.

Weather and Seasons

Have you ever wondered why the weather is the way it is? In this section, you'll learn why the seasons happen and the differences between them. And you'll understand where rain comes from, what snow is, how water freezes, and why you sometimes see and hear thunder and lightning.

Materials Around You

Look around! Everything you see is made of something—and that something is called a material. In this section you'll explore where materials come from, what they are used for, and what happens to them when they are heated or when they freeze.

When you see a word in **bold**, that means it's a science word. You'll find an explanation in the glossary at the back of the book on page 94.

Living Things

Plants and animals are living things. All living things do three things—they move, grow, and **reproduce**.

Living things grow.

Animals have young. This baby orangutan will grow up to look like its parents.

Plants can move parts of themselves. Some flowers close up at night.

Plants make **seeds** that grow into new plants. This seedling will grow into a tree.

Animals can move around.

Is It Alive?

When things are living, we say they are **alive**. Some things were once alive, but they are not alive any more. Some things have never lived.

Which group does each of these things belong to?

Alive

Was alive in the past

Never lived

sheep

shell

trampoline

girl

dead fly

spider

flame

cloud

flower

teddy bear

skeleton

Plants Everywhere

Plants are living things with green parts. Most plants have leaves. They are found all over the Earth—even near the South Pole.

Some plants, such as trees, are very, very big.

beech tree

grass

Other plants are very, very small.

moss

These are plants you might see in the city.

plane tree

grass

daffodils

dandelion

Where Do I Grow?

A **habitat** is a place where a plant or animal lives naturally. Can you match each plant to the place where you think it grows?

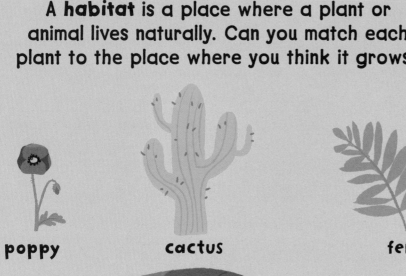

poppy

cactus

fern

coconut palm

woodland

meadow

hot island

desert

Plant Parts

Plants are made of different parts. Lots of plants have flowers. It's the flowers that make seeds!

A sunflower

Most flowers have bright petals, to attract insects.

The flower makes seeds, which grow into new plants.

Leaves soak up light and heat from the Sun, to make food.

The stem supports the plant, and carries water and **nutrients** from the soil around the plant.

Roots are shoots that anchor the plant in the ground and take in water and nutrients too.

Nutrients are substances that living things need to grow and to work properly.

Sunflowers face the Sun. They turn toward the Sun as it moves across the sky.

What Am I?

Read the captions and match them to the different parts of the plant.

We use light and heat to make food.

We hold the plant in the ground.

We attract insects.

seeds

flower

petal

We soak up water from the soil.

We help to make new plants.

leaf

I carry water from the ground around the plant.

We make seeds.

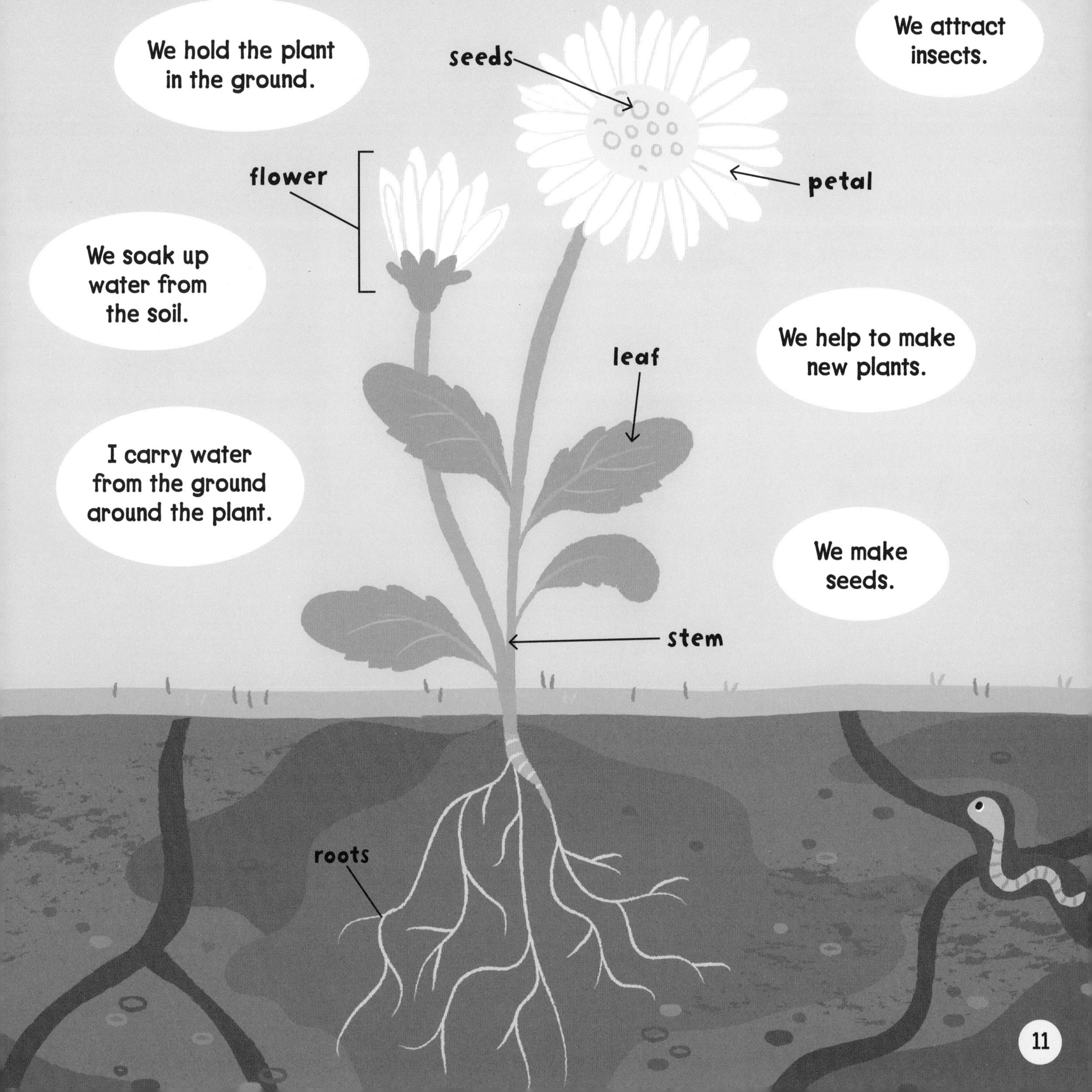

stem

roots

Wriggly Roots

Plants grow in many different places. The kind of roots a plant has depends on where it grows.

Carrots are small plants and don't need deep roots. They have a thick root called a taproot, which is the part that we eat.

Ivy grows on trees and other plants. It has roots in the ground, and little roots that grow in the air and help it to climb the tree.

This chestnut tree has wide, shallow roots that hold it steady in the ground. The roots soak up water and nutrients from the ground and carry them up to the tree trunk.

Tasty Taproots

Follow the routes to find out which vegetable each hungry creature will eat.

potatoes

beet

carrot

How Plants Grow

All plants need water, heat, and light from the Sun, plus **nutrients** from soil, to grow.

Light

Plants cannot grow in a dark place. They need light from the Sun.

Time

It takes many years for a tree to grow!

Warmth

Plants grow best when it is warm. They get heat from the Sun.

Air

Plants need to breathe, just like you!

Fungi

Mushrooms and other **fungi** help tree roots to absorb nutrients from the soil.

Water

Trees and other plants take in water from the soil through their roots.

Help Me Grow!

What does this little tomato plant need to help it grow? What are the things it does not need?

soil

butterfly

blackbird

sunshine

tomato

trowel

milk

carton of milk

horse

Mighty Trees

Trees come in all shapes and sizes, and they can live for a very long time —even thousands of years. Most trees have flowers, but not all.

Some trees keep their leaves all year round. These are **evergreen** trees. The giant redwood is an evergreen.

Some trees lose their leaves in winter. These are called **deciduous** trees. The oak tree is deciduous.

Evergreen trees often have very thin leaves called needles. The **fruit** of the redwood is called a cone. When it opens, seeds are released.

Deciduous trees often have broad, green leaves. The fruit of the oak tree is a nut called an acorn. It has a seed inside.

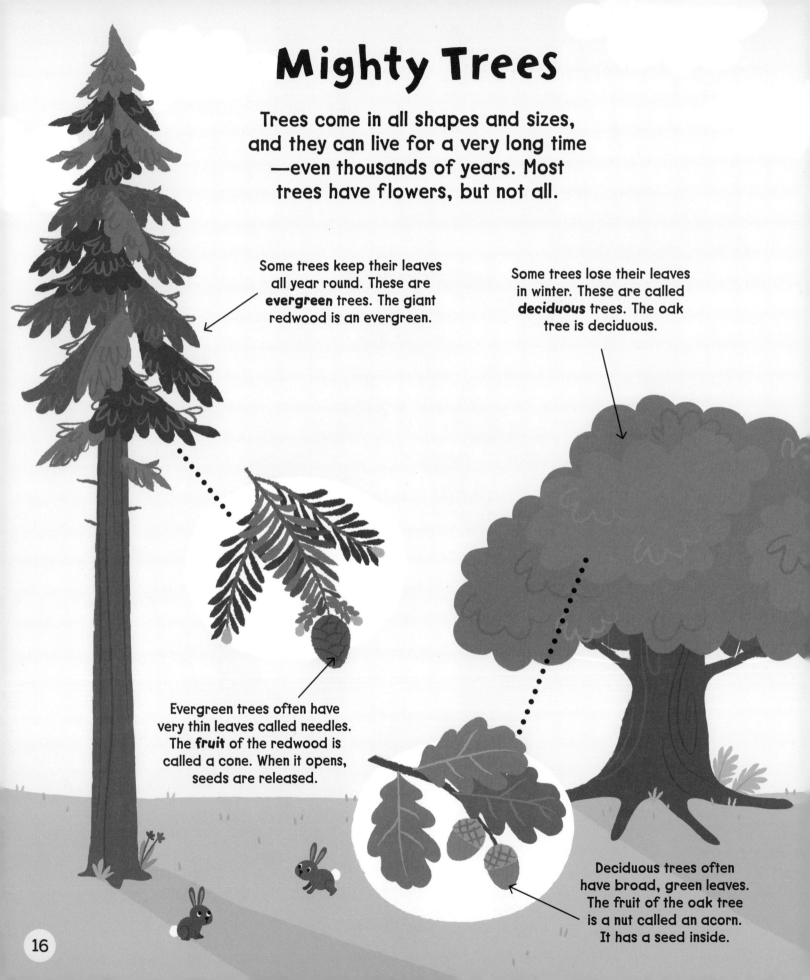

Falling Leaves

Look closely at the leaves.
Can you tell which ones come from
deciduous trees, and which ones
come from evergreen trees?

maple

Scots pine

ash

monkey
puzzle

yew

ginkgo

horse chestnut

Lebanese cedar

Super Seeds

Most plants reproduce by making seeds. Some seeds fall from their parents and land close by, then they take root and grow. Other seeds are blown away by the wind. Animals and birds also pick up seeds and carry them far away.

The seed of the horse chestnut tree is inside the shell.

Some fruits have seeds inside. Birds eat the fruit and fly away. Later, they pass the seeds out in their poop! The seeds land and grow into new plants.

The seed of the sycamore tree is carried away on the wind. It twists and spins in the air, landing far from the parent tree.

The seed falls from the tree and lands on the ground below.

The seed grows into a seedling, which eventually grows into a new horse chestnut tree!

Dandelion seeds blow away in the wind, and grow into new dandelions far away.

From Seed to Plant

Can you figure out which seed grows into which plant? Follow the dotted lines to find out.

oak tree

sunflower seed

acorn

pea plant

apple seed

pea

apple tree

sunflower

Fruit and Veg

Many animals (including people) eat plants. We don't always eat the whole plant—some parts are tastier than others. Different creatures like different bits!

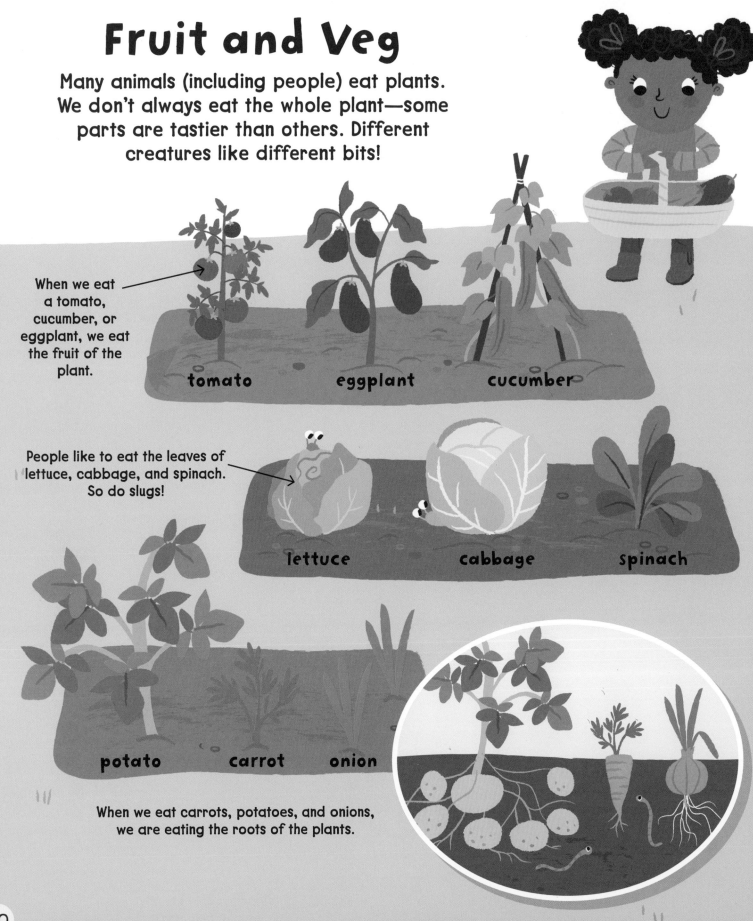

When we eat a tomato, cucumber, or eggplant, we eat the fruit of the plant.

tomato

eggplant

cucumber

People like to eat the leaves of lettuce, cabbage, and spinach. So do slugs!

lettuce

cabbage

spinach

potato   carrot   onion

When we eat carrots, potatoes, and onions, we are eating the roots of the plants.

Shopping Time

Leila is buying fruit and Tom is buying vegetables. They each have something in their basket that doesn't belong there. Can you tell what it is?

Habitat is Home

All living things live somewhere—that place is called their habitat. Some places are cold and wet, others are hot and dry. Most habitats are full of plants and animals that depend on each other. They are adapted to the place where they live.

Bluebells and primroses grow in the shaded woods.

Ferns, mosses, and mushrooms all like damp, shady places.

Mice live in underground burrows.

Rabbits also live in underground burrows.

A fox's home is underground. It's called a den.

Birds nest in trees.

Squirrels live in trees.

A very small place where many creatures live (like this log) is called a microhabitat.

Woodlice like dark, damp places.

Worms dig down into the soil.

Snails like to hide under leaves.

Help, We're Lost!

There has been a strange mix-up and the animals are not in their proper habitats! Can you put them back where they belong?

desert

cow

field

scorpion

river

trout

mossy log

beetle

ice floe

frog

tree

thrush

pond

penguin

Food Chain

All living things need food to stay alive. A **food chain** shows the connection between plants, animals, and food. The food chain always starts with a plant.

People eat fish. So do birds.

Animals that eat only meat are called **carnivores**.

Animals that eat plants and other animals are called **omnivores**.

Frogs, birds, and small fish eat insects.

Birds and small fish eat tadpoles.

Small fish and birds eat snails.

Snails and tadpoles eat plants.

Animals that eat only plants are called herbivores.

Birds and big fish eat small fish.

Eat or Be Eaten!

Each of these rows is a food chain, where one animal eats a plant or another animal. Can you place everything in the correct order? Clue: Each row starts with a plant.

a
blackbird
lettuce
slug

b
acorn
fox
squirrel

c
boy
grass
cow

d
trout
pondweed
stickleback

Animal Kingdom

There are all kinds of incredible animals living on the planet (and you are one of them!). Scientists divide animals into two main groups: animals with backbones and animals without backbones.

Invertebrates are animals that don't have a backbone.

A beetle belongs to the insect famiy.

A spider is an **arachnid**.

Worms are some of the most common invertebrates.

A snail is a kind of **mollusk**.

A crab is a **crustacean**.

An octopus is a mollusk.

Vertebrates are animals that do have a backbone.

A turtle is a **reptile**.

A frog is an **amphibian**.

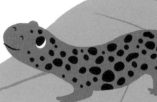

A rook is a bird.

A salamander is an amphibian.

A giraffe is a **mammal**.

A carp is a fish.

Human beings are mammals. Dogs are mammals too.

Rumble in the Jungle

All of these animals belong to one of the groups at the bottom of the page. Can you place each animal in the right group?

human

sloth

squirrel monkey

toucan

howler monkey

leopard

giant marauder ant

caiman

smoky jungle frog

poison arrow frog

discus fish

catfish

Insects have 6 legs.

Spiders have 8 legs.

Mollusks are animals with soft bodies. Most mollusks have shells.

Fish have wet scales and lay eggs in water.

wandering spider

red ants

parrot

tanager

tree boa

giant snail

horn snail

turtle

anteater

tree frog

chameleon

beetle

tarantula

apple snail

bird-eating spider

Birds have wings and feathers. They lay eggs.

Amphibians have moist skin and lay eggs in water.

Mammals have hair or fur. They have warm bodies. They feed their babies milk.

Reptiles have dry scales. Some reptiles have shells.

Creepy Crawlies

Most of the animals on Earth are invertebrates. They do not have a backbone, or spine, to protect them. Some invertebrates have a hard frame on the outside of their bodies, called an **exoskeleton**.

An insect has 6 legs, and its body is in 3 sections. It has an exoskeleton. Many insects have wings and can fly.

A spider has 8 legs and its body is in 2 sections. It has an exoskeleton.

All invertebrates lay eggs.

A worm is soft. It is an invertebrate but it doesn't have a skeleton.

A snail is a **mollusk**. It has a hard shell to protect its soft body.

Insect or Spider?

Do you know your insects from your spiders? Look carefully and see how many spiders you can find hidden here.

Beautiful Birds

All **birds** have feathers,
wings, two legs, and a beak.
They all lay eggs.
Most birds can fly!

A woodpecker uses its sharp beak for pecking wood to find food or to make a home.

An eagle catches food with its sharp talons.

A peacock spreads its beautiful tail feathers to attract a peahen.

A duck has webbed feet to paddle in water.

The kingfisher has strong, light feathers, which are perfect for flying and diving.

Perfectly Suited

Birds are adapted to the places where they live and the food they need to catch. Look at the pictures below and find the correct work to complete each sentence opposite.

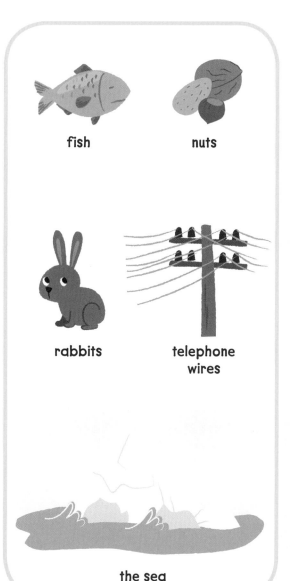

fish

nuts

rabbits

telephone wires

the sea

1 Penguins have webbed feet to help them swim in...

2 Gannets have long, thin, jagged beaks, great for catching slippery...

3 Bald eagles have sharp talons adapted to catch fish and furry...

4 Macaws have sharp, hooked bills, to help them crack hard...

5 Swallows have tiny feet, ideal for gripping thin branches, or...

Fishy Business

All fish have fins and their bodies are covered with wet scales. Fish cannot breathe air, or **oxygen**, the way you do. They breathe water, instead. Most fish live in the sea which is salty. Some fish prefer freshwater rivers and lakes.

swordfish

lionfish

Many fish live on or around coral reefs.

Some fish live in large groups called shoals. They live in the open ocean.

shoal of mackerel

seahorse

angel fish

frilled shark

viperfish

angler fish

tripod fish

The bottom of the ocean is a very dark place, but fish do live there. Some fish can make light by themselves.

Sea Food

There are food chains in the sea as well as on land. Look at these animals. Can you place them in size order, showing which one eats the next?

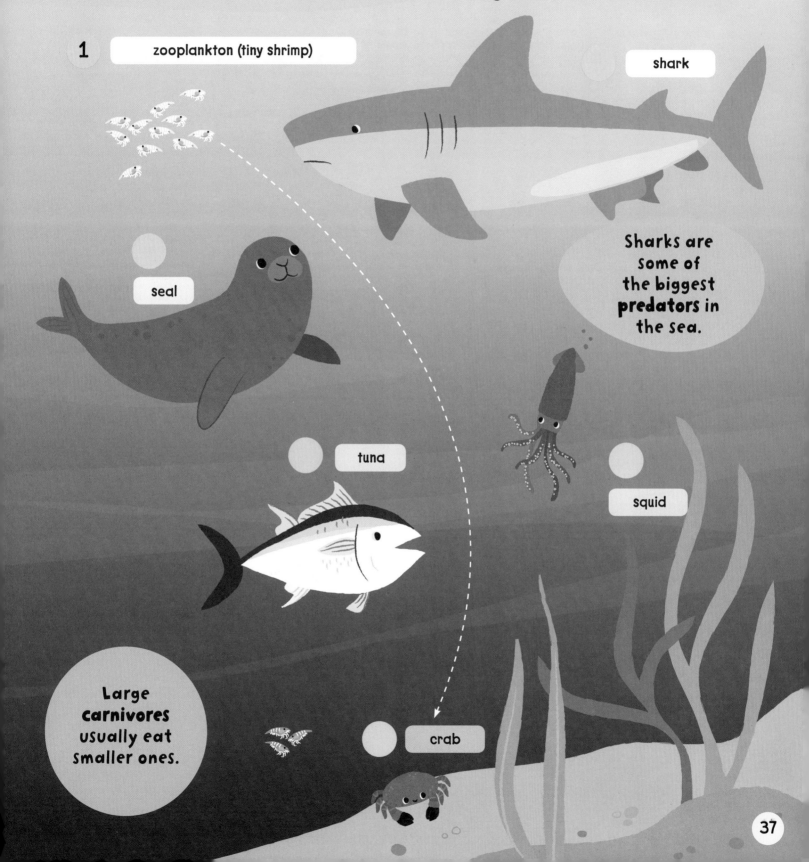

1 zooplankton (tiny shrimp)

shark

seal

Sharks are some of the biggest **predators** in the sea.

tuna

squid

Large **carnivores** usually eat smaller ones.

crab

Reptiles and Amphibians

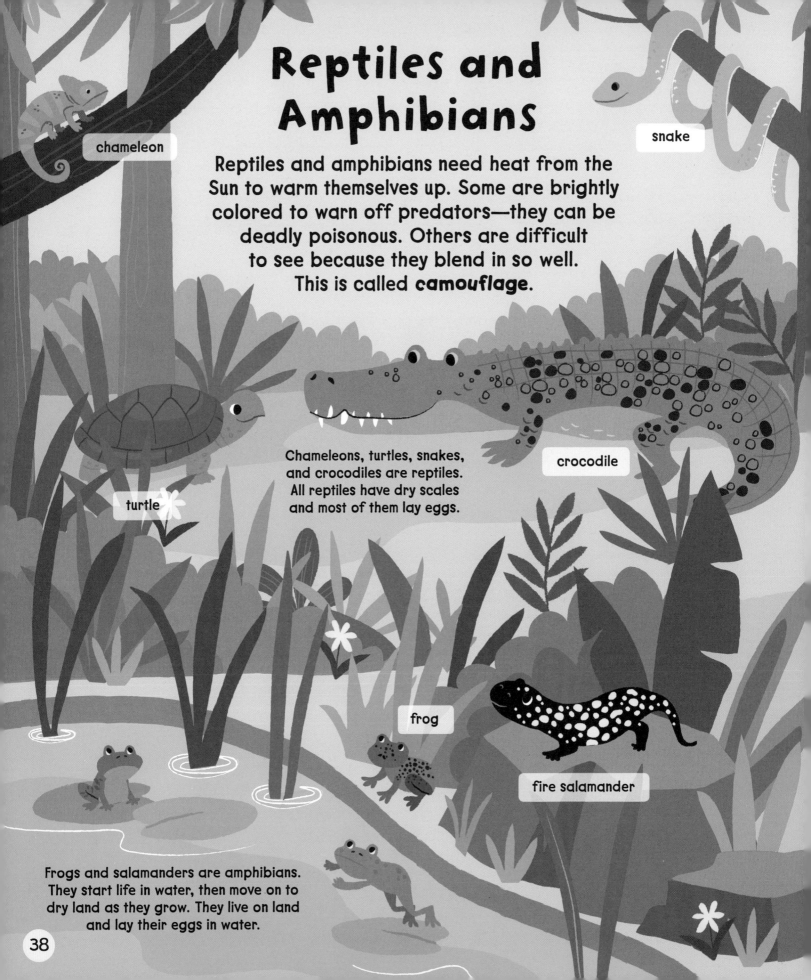

chameleon

snake

Reptiles and amphibians need heat from the Sun to warm themselves up. Some are brightly colored to warn off predators—they can be deadly poisonous. Others are difficult to see because they blend in so well. This is called **camouflage**.

Chameleons, turtles, snakes, and crocodiles are reptiles. All reptiles have dry scales and most of them lay eggs.

turtle

crocodile

frog

fire salamander

Frogs and salamanders are amphibians. They start life in water, then move on to dry land as they grow. They live on land and lay their eggs in water.

Spikes, Spots, and Stripes

Look at the animals and match them to the speech bubble that best describes their appearance.

eyelash viper

> I like to hide in shrubs and sand, and the spikes on my body protect me from being eaten.

Tonkin buck-eyed frog

> Pretending to be a thick, green vine in a tree helps me chase my food.

gila monster

> My tough, jagged shell protects me from other predators.

> My sandy, earthy patterns camouflage me as I slither over prairies.

thorny devil

> The dark, scaly patterns on my body help me blend into shadows in the desert.

snapping turtle

> I'm very tiny, but predators know not to eat me because I look bright and poisonous.

> My bright scales warn other animals to keep away.

emerald tree boa

> I like to spend my time near water pretending to be a mossy rock.

bullsnake

blue jeans frog

Mighty Mammals

Mammals have hair or fur (and sometimes prickles), and feed their babies with their own milk.

The porcupine has a coat of spiky prickles to protect it against predators.

A tiger's stripy fur helps it to hide in long grass.

The echidna has fur and spiky spines to protect itself. It's a very rare mammal that lays eggs.

Human beings are mammals. Most people have lots of hair on their head.

A dolphin is a mammal that lives in water. Dolphins are born with hair, but it drops out.

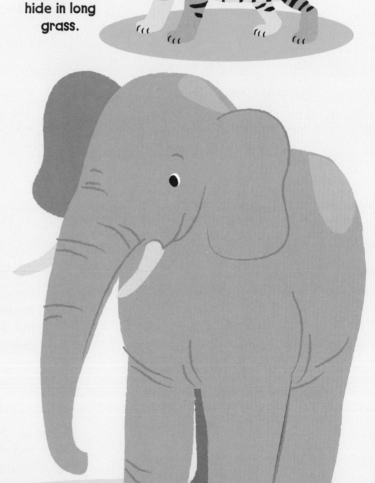

A mouse is a very small mammal with fur and a long tail.

The elephant is the largest mammal on dry land.

Find the Baby

The mothers have lost their babies. Can you help each baby find its mommy?

calf

bear

goat

baby

pinkie

human

joey

pup

camel

mouse

cub

seal

kid

kangaroo

41

Life Cycle

All animals have babies. This is called reproduction. Babies often look like their parents, but not always. Some animals go through huge changes as they grow.

Here is the life cycle of a frog. A baby frog, or tadpole, looks very different to an adult frog.

A female frog lays her eggs in water.

The tadpole grows into a frog.

The eggs grow into embryos. Little tails start to appear.

The tadpole grows four legs.

The tadpole gradually grows legs and loses its tail.

As an embryo develops, it hatches into a tadpole and swims in the water.

Eggstraordinary!

Some of these animals lay eggs, but not all!
Tick the box next to those that do.
Which animals are left?

beetle ☐

moth ☐

spider ☐

toad ☐

parrot ☐

polar bear ☐

tortoise ☐

rat ☐

giraffe ☐

donkey ☐

human ☐

Your Amazing Body

See how many parts of your body you can name.

Human beings are mammals, which means you can do amazing things! You grow, move around, explore, sleep, breathe ... and dance!

nose

head

eye

finger

hair

hand

wrist

ear

face

mouth

neck

elbow

chest

arm

thumb

knee

leg

ankle

toes

foot

Clever Senses

Your senses are working all the time, telling your body about the world around you. You can see, hear, smell, touch, and taste. Link the phrase to the part of the body that does the sensing.

a We can feel if something is hot or cold, hard or soft.

b We hear sounds that are very quiet or very loud.

c We see things up close and far away.

d I smell if something is good or bad.

e I tell you if something tastes good, or if it's bitter or sweet.

f We keep listening while you sleep!

Your Daily Plate

Your body is made of thousands of different parts all working together day and night. What your body needs most to stay fit and healthy is a variety of foods and lots of exercise.

You need lots of brown bread, pasta, porridge, rice, or potatoes every day for energy.

This plate shows you how much of each kind of food you should eat each day.

Eat at least 5 portions a day of vegetables and fruit.

Eat candies, cookies, and cakes in only small amounts. These are not good for you.

Cheese, milk, and eggs help your bones to grow strong.

Beans, pulses, fish, and meat are good for you. Try to eat fish twice a week.

Exercise builds strong muscles and bones, which is important when you are growing. Exercise makes your heart stronger too.

Do I or Don't I?

You only have one body and it's got to last your whole life! Take this test and see if you know how to look after yourself!

1

You've come home from school and you're a bit dirty. Your parents say it's dinnertime! Do you...

A) Sit down straight away?

B) Wash your hands and then sit down?

C) Wipe your nose on your sleeve and hope no one noticed?

2

You've worked on your spellings— well done! As a reward, you want to...

A) Watch your favorite TV show—it's only on once a week.

B) Listen to to a bedtime story.

C) Play computer games for two hours before bedtime.

3

You had PE today and your knees don't look very clean! Do you...

A) Cover them up and hope no one notices!

B) Have a shower?

C) Tell Dad not to worry, you'll scrub your knees with his toothbrush in the morning?

4

It's important on a school night to...

A) Read under the duvet with a torch until you fall asleep.

B) Try to get at least 10 hours sleep every night.

C) Stay up as late as possible—sleep is for losers!

5

You're in your PJs and ready for bed. There's just one more thing to do. Is it...

A) Kiss teddy goodnight?

B) Brush your teeth?

C) Hide under your little sister's bed and make monster noises?

Ages and Stages

As we grow up, we go through different life stages. We all began life growing inside our mothers.

Fetus

A baby grows inside its mother for 9 months before it is born.

Newborn

A newborn baby cannot do anything for herself. She depends on her parents for food, warmth, protection, and love.

Age 3

A young toddler can walk and is exploring the world. He is starting to feed himself but still needs his parents.

Age 5

At 5 years of age a child is ready to go to school. He is more independent and can feed himself and get dressed.

Age 13

This child is at the beginning of adolescence. Her body will go through lots of changes as she grows into an adult.

Age 18

This boy is an adult now and has started to grow hair on his face. He can look after himself.

Age 32

By the time she is 32, a girl has become a woman. She may be expecting a baby of her own.

Age 75

This is an old man. He only has a little hair and needs glasses to see more clearly.

Growing Up Tangle

How well do you know your ages and stages? Follow the lines to link the description with the right age.

Age 3

I'm a grown-up! And I'm growing a beard.

I haven't even been born yet!

I'm only a few days old. I can't do anything for myself.

Aged 75

Age 32

I've lived a long life. My eyesight isn't as good as it used to be.

Wow! The world is an amazing place. I want to explore it all the time!

Newborn

Fetus

Age 13

Age 18

I'm a woman now and may be having a baby of my own.

I'm not quite an adult yet. My body is still growing and changing.

Seasons

Throughout the year, there are times when the weather gets hotter, colder, or wetter. These are the seasons and they happen because the Earth tilts slightly as it travels around the Sun.

Winter in the Northern Hemisphere

When the northern part of Earth tilts away from the Sun, it receives less heat and light and so it is colder. Then it is wintertime in the North and summer in the South.

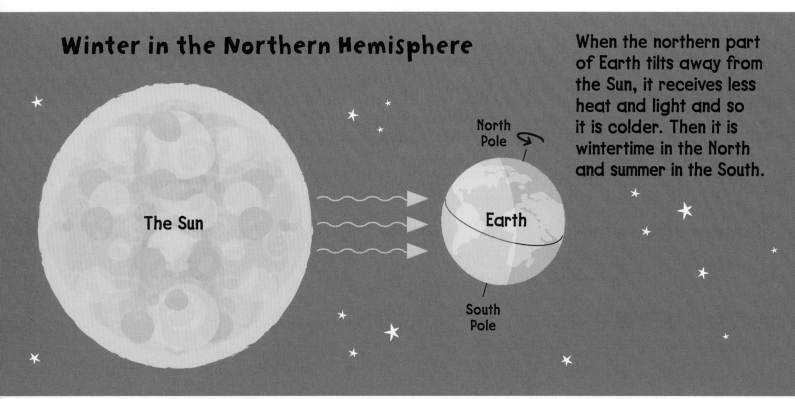

The Sun

North Pole

Earth

South Pole

Summer in the Northern Hemisphere

When the northern part of Earth tilts toward the Sun, it receives more heat and light and so it is warmer. Then it is summertime in the North.

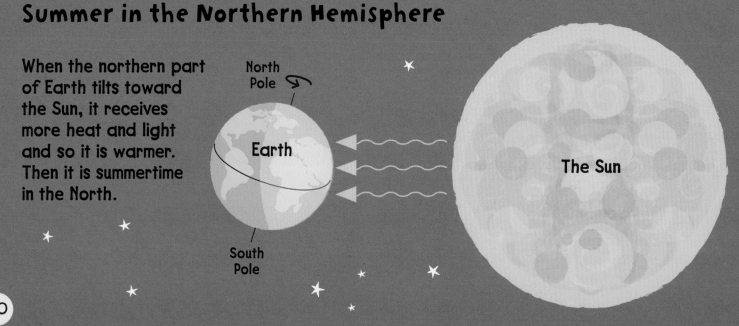

North Pole

Earth

South Pole

The Sun

Look Up!

When you get out of bed in the morning and look up at the sky, what you see is the weather. Look at these pictures and match them to the descriptions at the bottom of the page.

a

b

c

d

e

f

Stormy

Cold but not Snowing

Cold and windy

Raining

Cold and Snowing

Warm and Sunny

Spring Has Sprung!

In spring, the days grow longer and the weather begins to warm up. There is a lot of rain and everything starts to grow!

Apple blossom appears on apple trees.

New leaves unfold on the trees.

In spring, the Sun still lies low in the sky.

Birds lay eggs in their nests.

Lambs and other baby animals are born in spring.

Lambs and other baby animals are born in spring.

Daffodils and tulips bloom in spring.

What Season Am I?

Look at the pictures below and describe what you see. Which pictures show spring? What seasons do the other pictures show?

Hooray for Summer

In summertime, the days are long and the weather is warm and sunny. Trees are full of leaves and flowers grow.

Apples are growing on the tree.

Trees are covered with leaves.

Baby chicks are looked after by their parents.

The Sun is high in the sky.

Lambs grow bigger and stronger.

Crops grow in the field.

The rabbit kittens have also grown.

Lots of flowers and plants grow.

It's hot and sunny outside.

What's the Weather?

Can you answer the questions about the weather? Use the weather report to help you.

WEATHER REPORT

	Monday	Tuesday	Wednesday	Thursday	Friday	Saturday	Sunday
morning	☀️	❄️	☀️	☁️	☁️	🌧️	☀️
afternoon	☀️	❄️	☁️	☁️	☀️	☁️	☀️
evening	☀️	❄️	🌧️	⛈️	☁️	☀️	❄️
nighttime	❄️	❄️	🌧️	🌧️	🌧️	☁️	❄️

1   Which day was the sunniest?

2   Which day was the snowiest?

3   What season might this week be?

4   Is there more rain or more snow this month?

5   What was special about Thursday?

Fabulous Fall

Fall days grow shorter. The weather becomes cooler and there is more wind and rain. Trees start to lose their leaves and plants stop growing.

Birds leave the nest. Many fly south in winter.

Leaves change color and then fall to the ground.

The Sun lies lower in the sky.

Crops in the field have been harvested.

Sheep grow thick coats for the winter ahead.

Ripe apples are picked in September. If not, they fall off the trees!

The weather turns cold and it's time to wrap up warm again.

Pumpkin Patch

Help Larry Trotter wave his wand and arrange the images in the correct order, to show how a pumpkin grows from a seed to a big, ripe, orange fruit.

Winter Wonderland

In winter, the days are short and the weather turns cold. In some places, it even snows. Deciduous trees lose their leaves and flowers die.

The winter Sun is low in the sky.

Winter is a good time to put out seeds for little birds.

The fields are bare and covered with snow.

The branches of the trees are all bare.

All the flowers have died. The ground is covered in a blanket of snow.

Lend Nature a Hand

Birds and animals need different things in winter. Can you figure out what each animal needs?

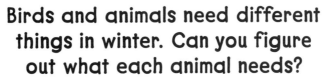

I like fruit and nuts. I bury some of my food and then dig it up in winter.

squirrel

pond

bird feeder

fruit and nuts

I'd like something long and crunchy to eat.

robin

I need a place where I can curl up in ball and sleep.

hedgehog

I like wet places.

frog

dead leaves

Whatever the Weather

Weather may be hot, cold, windy, or thundery. Weather changes with the seasons, and from country to country.

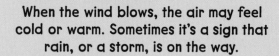

When the wind blows, the air may feel cold or warm. Sometimes it's a sign that rain, or a storm, is on the way.

On a sunny day in summer, the air feels hot.

In wintertime, the weather can be cold and icy.

When it's very cloudy, some clouds may reach the ground—that's fog!

When the weather is ice cold, rain turns to hail.

When clouds appear, they often bring rain and wet weather.

What to Wear

We wear certain clothes depending on the weather. Can you tell which clothes go with rain, sun, or snow?

1

2

rain

3

4

5

sun

7

6

snow

9

8

Cloudy Day

Clouds are made of tiny drops of water. They are constantly changing and moving across the sky.

Thin, wispy clouds high in the sky are made of ice.

On a fine, sunny day, you may see clouds that look like fluffy balls of cotton wool.

Low, dark clouds may be a sign that it's going to rain. They may hide more clouds above.

Fog is cloud that forms near the ground. If you walk through fog, you're walking through a cloud!

Weather Words

Some of these words describe the weather, and others don't. Can you circle all of the weather words?

quiet

cloudy

icy

drizzle

rainy

windy

hot

stripy

leafy

misty

noisy

breezy

blue

foggy

cold

snowy

freezing

smelly

Thunder and Lightning

When rain clouds darken overhead, there is a good chance that a thunderstorm is on the way. Thunder is the loud crashing noise you hear in the sky after lightning strikes!

Lightning is a flash of electricity that happens during thunderstorms. Light flashes between the clouds or travels down toward the ground.

Thunder is the sound made by a bolt of lightning.

Fine to Fly?

Up, up, and away!

Imagine that you're a pilot. Would it be safe for you to fly today? Look out of the window, and then follow the arrows below.

Watch out for heavy rain.

A dusting of light cloud just ahead.

Uh oh, thunder and lightning forecast!

Clear blue skies this way.

Fog and mist incoming. Watch out!

Oh no, dark clouds ahead!

Fluffy clouds up above.

Not safe to fly!

Hold on to your hat, it's windy up there!

Very calm, no wind, the coast is clear!

WHAT'S THE WEATHER LIKE TODAY?

START HERE!

The Water Cycle

The **water cycle** is the constant journey that water makes from the sea to the sky above, and back again. It's very important for life on Earth. Without it, nothing would grow and we couldn't live.

When water warms up, it turns into a gas, called water vapor. This is known as **evaporation**.

Water vapor rises into the sky.

As water vapor rises, it starts to cool down. It turns back into drops of water and forms clouds.

When water vapor turns back into liquid water, this is called **condensation**.

The Sun heats up seawater and water in rivers and lakes.

Wind blows clouds over land and sea. Water held in the clouds falls as rain.

When the temperature is freezing, water in the clouds falls as snow or hail.

Water that falls as rain, snow, hail, or sleet, is called **precipitation**.

Rain falls on plants and on the ground. It flows into rivers and lakes.

Water flows from rivers and lakes back to the sea.

Water seeps down through layers of soil and rock and travels underground toward the sea.

Water Cycle Game

Now it's time for you to play water cycle snakes and ladders. All you need is a couple of friends, a die, and a few buttons to use as markers.

81	82	83	84	85
80	79	78	77	76
61	62 Condensation	63	64	65
60	59	58	57	56 Evaporation
41	42	43 Precipitation	44	45
40	39	38	37	36
21	22	23	24	25
20	19 Condensation	18	17	16
Start 1	2	3	4	5

Rules

Each player places their counter on the start. The aim is to reach the Finish first.

 Warm water rises and turns in to water vapor. Rise up to the square above!

 The Sun heats up water. Have another go!

 You've landed on a snow cloud. Take shelter from the cold by moving back 5 squares.

 Uh-oh, it's raining. Fall down to the square below.

 You've hit a snowy peak! Fall down 2 squares.

 Here comes the wind to blow you along. Fast forward 5 squares.

If you land on a square with a word, say what the word means. If you're right, have another go. If you get it wrong, you miss a turn.

86	87	88	89	Finish
75 Precipitation	74	73	72	71
66	67	68	69	70
55	54	53	52 Condensation	51
46	47	48	49	50
35	34	33 Precipitation	32	31
26 Evaporation	27	28	29	30
15	14	13	12	11
6	7	8	9	10

Marvelous Materials

Look at the things around you. They are all made of something, and that something is called a **material**. There are lots of different kinds of materials.

 This is a chair. →  It is made of wood. → Wood comes from trees.

 This is a can. It is made from a mixture of metals. → Metals come from rocks, called **ore**. →  Rocks are dug up from the ground.

 These are a pair of glasses. →  Glass is made of sand. →  Sand comes from the sea, beaches, dunes, and rocks.

 This is a pair of denim jeans. →  Denim is made of cotton. → Cotton comes from a plant.

 This is a jug. → The jug is made from clay. → 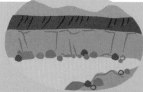 Clay is a type of rocky soil dug from the ground.

Where Did It Come From?

Can you guess what material each object is made from?

a

b

c

d

e

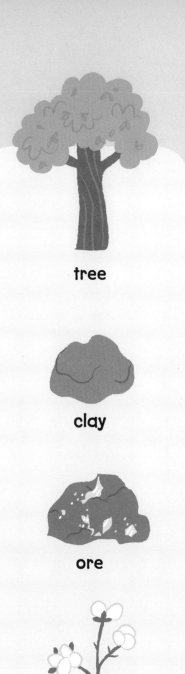

tree

clay

ore

cotton

sand

More Marvelous Materials

Some materials are better for making certain things than others.

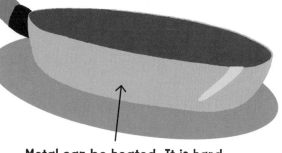

Wool comes from sheep. It is stretchy, soft, and warm, which makes it perfect for clothes.

Metal can be heated. It is hard-wearing and difficult to break, so it will last a long time.

Glass is hard, see-through, and waterproof, which makes it perfect for a fish tank.

Clay is soft when it comes out of the earth. It can be shaped easily. When it is baked, it becomes very hard. Clay is used for lots of things, but it makes great plant pots.

Build Me!

What would you use to make the things that are labeled on this house? Choose the best material from the objects in the panel below.

drainpipe

roof

wall

veranda

door

slate   bricks   straw   wood   stone   sticks   plastic

Look Around

Take a look at your kitchen. Everything you see is made from one or more materials. Some materials are better than others—it depends what job you want them to do.

Glass is clear. You can see through it and it is smooth.

Rubber gloves are light, bendy, and waterproof.

Metal is strong. It won't break.

A wool sweater is soft and warm.

A stone counter is hard and won't scratch easily.

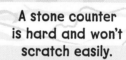

A plastic bowl is waterproof and strong. It won't leak and it won't break easily.

This wooden table is stiff, strong, and hard.

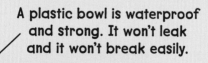

Think Like a Designer

Imagine you have a job designing everyday things. What do you think the following objects should be made from? Choose from the following: clay, cotton, metal, plastic, rubber, wood.

1

2

3

4

5

6

7

8

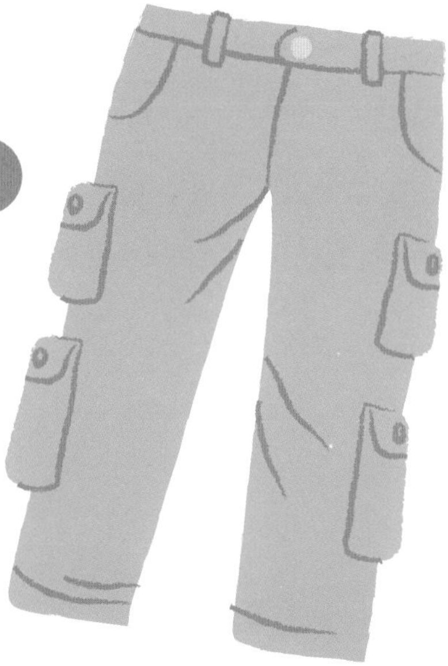

9

Changing Shape

You can change the shape of some materials. You can bend, twist, pull, stretch, or squash a material to suit your needs.

You can easily change the shape of paper: you can fold it or scrunch it.

An elastic band stretches, then goes back to its original length when you let go.

You can twist and bend this desk light so the light shines where you want it to.

When you squash a teddy bear, it changes shape, but only for as long as you hold it.

Find the Words

Look at this selection of everyday things. Draw a line between the objects to the word that best describes how you can change their shape!

Wool scarf

Coat hanger

Cotton sweatshirt

Earphones

Springy toys

Fluffy socks

Rubber boots

twist   **stretch**   **squash**   **bend**

Solids, Liquids, and Gases

All materials can be described as one of these three things: a **solid**, **gas**, or **liquid**.

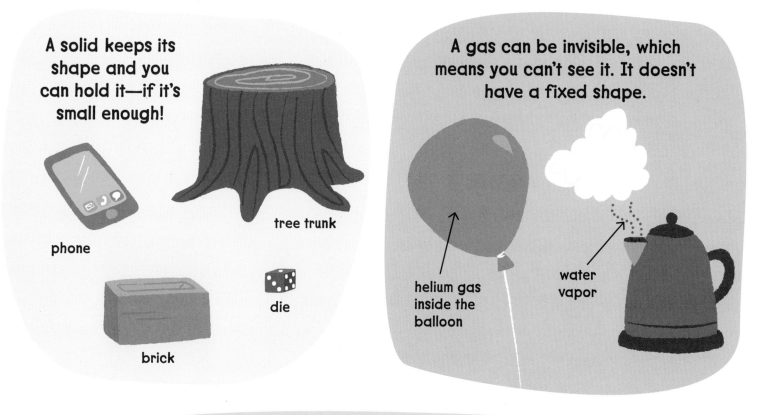

A solid keeps its shape and you can hold it—if it's small enough!

phone

tree trunk

brick

die

A gas can be invisible, which means you can't see it. It doesn't have a fixed shape.

helium gas inside the balloon

water vapor

A liquid flows and can be poured easily. It is not easy to hold. It changes shape to fill the container it is in.

water

juice

custard

Help the Teacher

The teacher is trying to explain the differences between liquids, solids, and gases. Can you draw a line from each object to the correct heading?

Liquid **Solid** **Gas**

exhaust fumes

milk

runny honey

wooden spoon

hair clip

cookin gas

tea

breaking wind!

bubbles in fizzy water

Fizzy Water

book

air

Heating Up, Cooling Down

Solids, liquids, and gases don't always stay the way they are. If you heat ice (a solid) it turns into water (a liquid). When the water (liquid) cools down and freezes, it turns back into ice (solid).

Heat turns liquid water into water vapor, which is a gas. Water vapor is invisible.

When water vapor touches the air, it cools down. It turns into tiny droplets of liquid water. This is steam.

A gas can become a solid too, when cold water vapor freezes on a window in winter.

If you heat some solids, they turn into liquids. Butter goes runny when you heat it.

Freezing and Melting

These penguins are experimenting with water and ice. Can you match the descriptions to each picture?

1

When ice melts, it turns to water.

2

When water freezes, it turns to ice.

Rocking Rocks

The Earth's surface is made of rock that lies just below the ground. People have been digging up rocks for thousands of years! There are many different kinds and some are harder than others.

Sandstone is good for building. It is soft enough to carve.

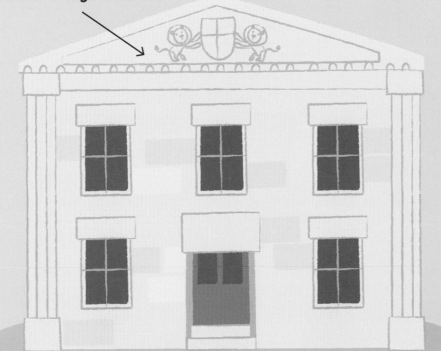

Marble is a beautiful, hard rock. It is good for sculpture and table tops.

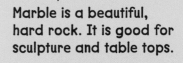

Chalk is a soft, white rock. It's perfect for writing and drawing on a blackboard!

Granite is a very hard rock made of differently shaded grains that have sharp edges.

The Right Rock

Look at the finished objects and see if you can figure out which kind of rock they are made from.

 **Chalk** is soft enough for writing.

 **Sandstone** is strong enough for building.

 **Marble** looks beautiful to artists.

 **Granite** is tough enough for walking on.

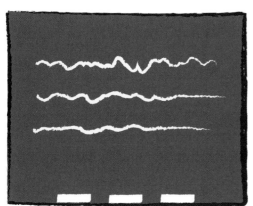

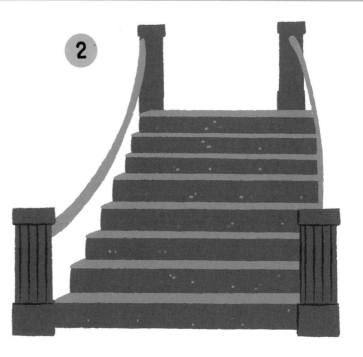

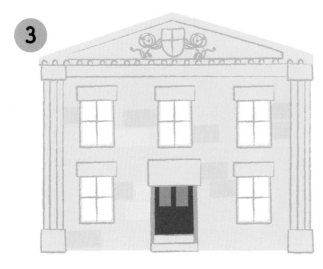

Simply Soil

Resting on top of all the rock on Earth is a layer of soil. Soil is made of bits of rock and dead plants, together with water, air, and tiny living creatures, such as animals and fungi. They all provide important things which help plants to grow.

The top layer is called the topsoil. It is usually dark brown. There are lots of bits of fungi, animals, and dead plants here.

The next layer is the subsoil. The subsoil doesn't have many dead plants. It has lots of clay and is usually light brown.

The layer called the parent rock has lots of stones. Very few dead plants are found here.

A layer called bedrock lies at the bottom. It is solid rock.

Clear as Mud!

The Earth is covered in many different kinds of soil, which help plants grow. Can you match the description to the picture?

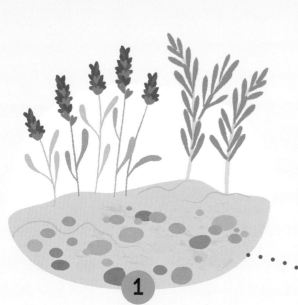

1

2

Peaty soil is dark brown and crumbly. It doesn't contain many stony bits. It's made from rotting plants from long ago.

Chalky soil is light brown. Water passes through it quickly.

Sandy soil is pale. It has chunky bits of rock in it and lots of air gaps. Water passes through it easily. It feels quite dry.

3

Clay soil is sticky and has small bits in it. There are very few air gaps. Water does not pass through it easily.

4

Dinosaur Bones

Fossils are the ancient remains of living things locked in stone. Fossils can be anything from tiny organisms to plants and the bones, teeth, and even eggs of animals. Fossils tell us what life was like on Earth millions of years ago.

These pictures show you how a dinosaur fossil formed millions of years ago.

1 This dinosaur is a Triceratops. It died of old age. The body is washed into the sea and sinks to the sea floor.

2 The body parts rot away and the skeleton sinks beneath the seabed. Layers of mud and silt build up, forcing out water. The layers harden and turn to stone. The skeleton turns to stone too and becomes a fossil.

Dinosaur experts are called **paleontologists** (say pale-ee-un-tol-o-jist). They are scientists who study what life was like on Earth millions of years ago. Because of their work, we know about Triceratops and all the other dinosaurs and ancient reptiles.

3 Over millions of years, the layers of rock move and change shape. Old rocks from deep inside the Earth are forced upward toward the surface. The fossilized Triceratops is carried up with them.

4 Over many more millions of years, the weather and the wind wear away rocks on the Earth's surface. Gradually, the fossilized bones are uncovered.

Fossil Hunters

Look at the fossils below. Some of them have been found in rocks that are more than 500,000 years old!

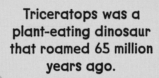

Triceratops was a plant-eating dinosaur that roamed 65 million years ago.

The brittle star fish lived 435 million years ago, and they still exists today. The first star fish may be even older.

Smilodon was a ferocious carnivore with huge fangs, that prowled the earth 2.5 million to 10,000 years ago.

Trilobites were marine invertebrates that looked like woodlice. They first swam in the seas more than 450 million years ago, but they're now extinct.

Crocodiles first appeared 200 million years ago. They outlived the dinosaurs!

The nautilus is an ancient sea creature that still swims in the Indian Ocean today. It first appeared over 500 million years ago.

The first fish lived more than 500 million years ago.

Now it's your turn to be a palaeontologist.
Can you draw a line from the fossil remains on the previous
page to the correct layer of rock? Look carefully and
you'll see clues.

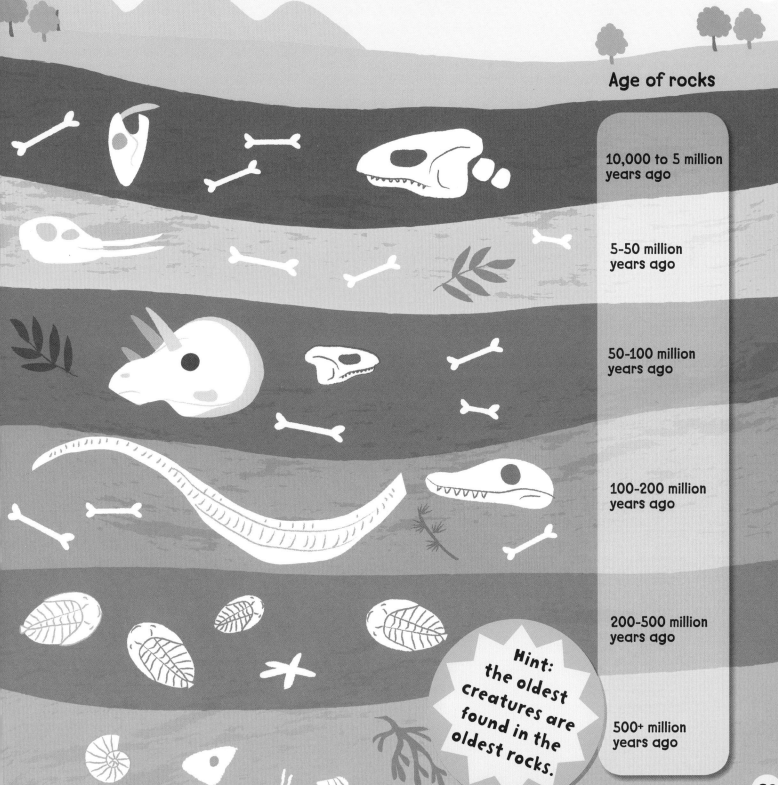

Age of rocks

10,000 to 5 million
years ago

5-50 million
years ago

50-100 million
years ago

100-200 million
years ago

200-500 million
years ago

Hint:
the oldest
creatures are
found in the
oldest rocks.

500+ million
years ago

ANSWERS

PAGE 7: Is It Alive?

Alive: sheep, spider, flower, girl

Never lived: teddy bear, cloud, flame, trampoline

Was alive in the past: shell, dead fly, skeleton

PAGE 9: Where Do I Grow?

Meadow—poppy
Hot island—coconut palm
Desert—cactus
Woodland—ferns

PAGE 11: What Am I?

We hold the plant in the ground —roots.

We soak up water from the soil —roots.

We help to make new plants— flower.

We use light, air, heat, and water to make food—leaves.

We make seeds—flower.

We attract insects—flower.

I carry water up from the ground to the plant—stem.

PAGE 13: Tasty Taproots!

PAGE 15: Help Me Grow!

The plant needs soil and sunshine. It doesn't need: blackbird, trowel, butterfly, horse, or carton of milk.

PAGE 17: Falling Leaves

Deciduous: maple, horse chestnut, ash, ginkgo

Evergreen: Scots pine, monkey puzzle, yew, Lebanese cedar

PAGE 19: From Seed to Plant

PAGE 21: Shopping Time

Leila's basket has fruit: apple, pineapple, strawberries, orange and a carrot (carrot is the odd one out)

Tom's basket has: potatoes, leeks, carrots, and tomatoes (tomatoes are the odd ones out)

PAGE 24-25: Help, We're Lost!

Ice floe—penguin

Mossy log—beetle

Field—cow

Tree—thrush

Desert—scorpion

River—trout

Pond with lily pad—frog

Page 27: Eat or Be Eaten!

a: lettuce, slug, blackbird

b: acorn, squirrel, fox

c: grass, cow, boy

d: pondweed, stickleback, trout

PAGE 30-31: Rumble in the Jungle

Insects: red ants, giant marauder ant, beetle

Spiders: tarantula, wandering spider, bird-eating spider

Mollusks: giant snail, horn snail, apple snail

Fish: catfish, discus fish

Birds: toucan, tanager, parrot

Amphibians: tree frog, poison arrow frog, smoky jungle frog

Mammals: human, sloth, squirrel monkey, leopard, howler monkey, anteater

Reptiles: turtle, caiman, chameleon, tree boa

PAGE 33: Insect or Spider?

PAGE 35: Perfectly Suited

Penguins have webbed feet to help them swim in the sea.

Gannets have long, thin, jagged beaks, great for catching slippery fish.

Bald eagles have sharp talons adapted to catch fish and furry rabbits.

Macaws have sharp, hooked bills, to help them crack hard nuts.

Swallows have tiny feet, ideal for gripping thin branches, or telephone wires.

PAGE 37: Sea Food

1. Zooplankton
2. Crab
3. Squid
4. Tuna
5. Seal
6. Shark

PAGE 39: Spikes, Spots and Stripes

Eyelash viper: My bright scales warn other animals to keep away.

Gila monster: The dark, scaly patterns on my body help me blend into shadows in the desert.

Blue jeans frog: I'm very tiny, but predators know not to eat me because I look bright and poisonous.

Snapping turtle: My tough, jagged shell protects me from other predators.

Thorny devil: I like to hide in shrubs and sand, and the spikes on my body protect me from being eaten.

Emerald tree boa: Pretending to be a thick, green vine in a tree helps me chase my food.

Bullsnake: My sandy, earthy patterns camouflage me as I slither over prairies.

Tonkin buck-eyed frog: I like to spend my time near water pretending to be a mossy rock.

PAGE 41: Find the Baby

Human and baby

Bear and cub

Camel and calf

Goat and kid

Kangaroo and joey

Mouse and pinkie

Seal and pup

PAGE 43: Eggstraordinary!

Do lay eggs—parrot, tortoise, moth, toad, spider, beetle

Don't lay eggs—donkey, rat, polar bear, giraffe, human

PAGE 45: Clever Senses

a. hand

b, f. ears

c. eyes

d. nose

e. tongue

PAGE 47: Do I or Don't I?

Mostly As) You know what you should do, but sometimes it's difficult doing the sensible thing. Always wash your hands before you eat and try to get a little more sleep every night!

Mostly Bs) You don't need any advice—you really know what's good for you. Well done!

Mostly Cs) Uh-oh, at this rate you will wear yourself out by the time you are 20! Remember to wash your hands, brush your teeth, and get plenty of sleep—you need it!

PAGE 49: Growing Up Tangle

PAGE 51: Look Up!

a. Cold and snowing.

b. Cold but not snowing.

c. Cold and windy.

d. Raining.

e. Stormy—it's raining.

f. Warm and sunny.

Page 53: What Season Am I?

a. Fall

b. Summer

c. Spring

d. Summer

e. Winter

f. Spring

PAGE 55: What's the Weather?

1. Monday

2. Tuesday

3. Winter

4. Snow

5. Lightning

PAGE 57: Pumpkin Patch

e, c, a, d, f, b

PAGE 59: Lend Nature a Hand

Bird feeder—robin

Pile of dead leaves—hedgehog

Nuts, carrots, apple—squirrel

Pond—frog

PAGE 61: What to Wear

Rain: 2, 4, 5

Sun: 1, 7, 8

Snow: 3, 6, 9

PAGE 63: Weather Words

Twelve weather words: hot, cold, rainy, windy, icy, snowy, drizzle, cloudy, breezy, misty, foggy, freezing

Six non-weather words: quiet, noisy, leafy, blue, smelly, stripy

PAGE 65: Fine to Fly?

Your answer will depend on the weather outside your window.

The statements along the right-hand side to the top will get you safely into the sky:

- Very calm, no wind, the coast is clear! - Fluffy clouds up above. - Clear blue skies this way. - A dusting of light cloud just ahead. - Up, up and away!

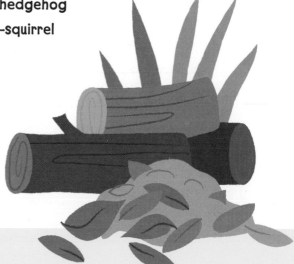

PAGE 71: Where Did You Come From?

(a) **Bricks**: clay

(b) **Wooden spoon**: tree

(c) **Pot**: ore (metal) – and the wooden handle came from a tree

(d) **Drinking glass**: sand

(e) **T-shirt**: cotton

PAGE 73: Build Me!

Roof—slate

Wall—bricks

Door, veranda—wood

Drainpipe—plastic

PAGE 75: Think Like a Designer

Most of the objects can be made from several different materials! Here is a suggestion.

1. Wood (paper)
2. Clay
3. Wood
4. Cotton
5. Wood
6. Metal and plastic
7. Cotton (and rubber)
8. Cotton
9. Metal

PAGE 77: Find the Words

Twist: wool scarf, springy toys, earphones

Stretch: cotton sweatshirt, fluffy socks, springy toys

Bend: rubber boots, coat hanger

Squash: fluffy socks, wool scarf

PAGE 79: Help the Teacher

Liquid: runny honey, milk, tea

Solid: wooden spoon, hair clip, book

Gas: exhaust fumes, cooking gas, bubbles in fizzy water, breaking wind, air

PAGE 81: Freezing and Melting

(1) When water freezes, it turns to ice.

(2) When ice melts, it turns to water.

PAGE 83: The Right Rock

Writing on a blackboard—chalk

Grand staircase—granite

Palace—sandstone

Sculpture—marble

PAGE 85: Clear as Mud!

Picture 1: Sandy soil

Picture 2: Clay soil

Picture 3: Chalky soil

Picture 4: Peaty soil

PAGE 88-89: Fossil Hunters

Triceratops: 50–100 million years ago

Brittle star fish: 200–500 million years ago

Smilodon: 10,000–5 million years ago

Trilobites: 200–500 million years ago

Crocodiles: 100–200 million years ago

Nautilus: 500+ million years ago

Fish: 500+ million years ago

GLOSSARY

Alive When things are living, they are alive.

Amphibian Animals that start life in water, then move on to dry land as they grow. They have moist skin and lay their eggs in water. Frogs, toads, newts, and salamanders are all amphibians.

Arachnid A type of invertebrate animal that lives on dry land and lay eggs. Arachnids are different from insects in that their bodies are made of two parts and they do not have wings. Most arachnids have eight legs. Spiders and scorpions are examples of arachnids.

Bird A type of egg-laying vertebrate. All birds have wings, feathers, two legs, and a beak. Most birds can fly. There are more than 10,000 kinds of birds.

Camouflage The natural coloring or shape of an animal that helps it to blend in with its surroundings.

Carnivore An animal that eats only other animals.

Condensation When a gas changes into a liquid. For example, when water vapor comes in to contact with cold air or a cold surface, it turns into drops of liquid water.

Crustacean A type of animal such as a crab, lobster, or shrimp. Most crustaceans live in the sea, but woodlice, for example, live on land.

Deciduous Trees that lose their leaves in winter.

Evaporation When a liquid changes into a gas. For example, when water warms up, it turns into a fine mist or gas, called water vapor.

Evergreen Trees that keep their leaves all year round.

Exoskeleton A hard frame or skeleton on the outside of the body of some invertebrate animals.

Food chain The relationship between what eats what, either on land or in the sea.

Fossil The ancient remains of animals, plants, and micro-organisms that once lived, preserved in rock.

Fruit The part of a plant that surrounds the seeds and can be eaten as food.

Fungi A living organism such as a mushroom, toadstool, yeast, and mold.

Gas A substance that is invisible and spreads out to fill the container that it is in. Oxygen, which is in the air, is a gas. Water vapor (before it turns into steam) is a type of gas.

Habitat The natural home of an animal, plant, or organism. A very small habitat, such as under a stone or a log, is called a microhabitat.

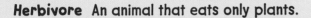
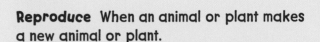

Herbivore An animal that eats only plants.

Invertebrate An animal that does not have a backbone or spine, and which lays eggs. Insects, mollusks, worms, crustaceans, and arachnids are all invertebrates.

Life cycle The changes that happen to a human, animal or plant as it grows older.

Liquid A substance that is runny and flows freely, like water or oil.

Mammal A vertebrate animal with hair, fur, or skin. Mammals feed their babies with their own milk. A few mammals, such as the echidna, lay eggs.

Material What things are made of. Metal, wood, clay, glass, and plastic are all materials.

Mollusk An invertebrate animal with a soft body. Most mollusks have shells.

Nutrients Substances that are very important for the growth and development of plants and animals.

Omnivore An animal that eats plants and other animals.

Ore A rock or natural material from which metal can be extracted.

Oxygen A natural gas in the air that is essential for all life on earth.

Precipitation Water that falls to the ground as rain, snow, hail, or sleet.

Predator An animal that eats other animals.

Reproduce When an animal or plant makes a new animal or plant.

Reptile A vertebrate animal that has dry scales. Some reptiles, such as turtles and tortoises, have shells. Most reptiles lay eggs.

Root The part of a plant that holds it in the soil, and takes in water and nutrients from the soil.

Seed The part of a plant that grows into a new plant.

Solid A substance that is hard and keeps its shape. A solid is difficult to squash.

Stem The part of a plant that supports the plant and carries water and nutrients up from the soil.

Vertebrate An animal that has a backbone or spine. Mammals (including humans), birds, reptiles, and fish are all vertebrates.

INDEX